Judy Gordon   Cy Coleman
Maurice & Lois F. Rosenfield
in association with Irvin Feld and Kenneth Feld
present

JIM DALE

in

Music by	Lyrics by	Book by
Cy Coleman	**Michael Stewart**	**Mark Bramble**

with

Glenn Close

Scenery Designed by	Costumes Designed by	Lighting Designed by	Sound Designed by
David Mitchell	**Theoni V. Aldredge**	**Craig Miller**	**Otts Munderloh**

Orchestrations by	Vocal Arrangements by		Music Director
Hershy Kay	**Cy Coleman** &	**Jeremy Stone**	**Peter Howard**

Directed and Staged by

Joe Layton

ISBN-13: 978-1-4234-2472-7
ISBN-10: 1-4234-2472-7

7777 W. BLUEMOUND RD. P.O. BOX 13819 MILWAUKEE, WI 53213

For info on Notable Music Co. Inc./The Cy Coleman Office, visit
www.cycoleman.com and www.myspace.com/cycoleman

Visit Hal Leonard Online at
www.halleonard.com

Cy Coleman

Cy Coleman was a musician's composer, classically trained at piano, composition, and orchestration at New York City's High School for the Performing Arts and NY College of Music. Mr. Coleman was being groomed to be the next great conductor. Instead he turned his passion to jazz and formed the popular Cy Coleman Trio. Born Seymour Kaufman on June 14, 1929 in the Bronx, he changed his name at age 16 in time to use it on his first compositions with lyricist Joe A. McCarthy ("Why Try to Change Me Now," and "I'm Gonna Laugh You Right out of My Life"). While still performing in jazz clubs and enjoying a successful recording career, Cy began writing with veteran songwriter Carolyn Leigh. Hits like "Witchcraft" and "The Best Is Yet to Come" were followed by their leap to Broadway with *Wildcat,* starring Lucille Ball ("Hey, Look Me Over") and then *Little Me* ("I've Got Your Number" and "Real Live Girl"). In 1966 Cy, along with legendary lyricist Dorothy Fields, triumphed with the smash hit *Sweet Charity* ("Big Spender," "If My Friends Could See Me Now"). Cy continued on Broadway and wrote the scores for *Seesaw, I Love My Wife, On the Twentieth Century, Barnum, City of Angels, The Will Rogers Follies,* and *The Life.* In 2004 Cy returned to his roots and revived the Cy Coleman Trio, once again wowing the audiences with his amazing skill at the piano. In Mr. Coleman's amazing career he took home three Tony® Awards, two GRAMMY Awards®, three Emmy® Awards, an Academy Award® nomination, and countless honors. Cy served on the Board of ASCAP for three decades.

Michael Stewart

Michael Stewart scored on Broadway the first time out when he won a Tony® Award for his *Bye Bye Birdie* libretto. He was the librettist for *Carnival* (Drama Critics Circle Award) and *Hello, Dolly!,* which won him both a Tony® Award and a Drama Critics prize. He also wrote the books for *George M!, Mack and Mabel,* and *The Grand Tour*; both book and lyrics for *I Love My Wife*; and lyrics for *Barnum.* Mr. Stewart died in 1987.

CONTENTS

THERE'S A SUCKER BORN
EV'RY MINUTE

Music by CY COLEMAN
Lyrics by MICHAEL STEWART

1. There is a suck-er _____ born ev-'ry min-ute, _____
2. Each bless-ed hour _____ brings six-ty of 'em _____
3. There is a suck-er _____ born ev-'ry min-ute, _____

THANK GOD I'M OLD

Music by CY COLEMAN
Lyrics by MICHAEL STEWART

slip back on the shelf ___ have a lit - tle nip and tell my - self, ___

Though my back buck - les and bends, ___ My hair got sil - ver - y ends, ___

When I see all of my friends ___ laid out and cold, ___

Thank God I'm Old. ___

THE COLORS OF MY LIFE

Music by CY COLEMAN
Lyrics by MICHAEL STEWART

14

ONE BRICK AT A TIME

Music by CY COLEMAN
Lyrics by MICHAEL STEWART

22

MUSEUM SONG

Music by CY COLEMAN
Lyrics by MICHAEL STEWART

Very bright

Quite a lot-ta
Ar-ma-dil-las,

Ro-man ter-ra cot-ta,
clev-er cat-er-pil-lars,

Liv-in' la-va from the
Re-pro-duc-tions of the

flanks of Et-na.
Cy-clops' ret-'na.

Stat-u-ar-y
Crys-tal blow-in',

ride a drom-e-dar-y,
au-to-mat-ic sew-in',

I LIKE YOUR STYLE

Music by CY COLEMAN
Lyrics by MICHAEL STEWART

We're out of step, we dis - a - gree,
When I pro - pose, then you pro - test,
Each bless - ed day we sweet - ly fill,

What's right for you _____ is wrong for me, To -
What's my de - light _____ you just de - test, Too
with "No you won't" _____ and "Yes you will, You

LOVE MAKES SUCH FOOLS OF US ALL

Music by CY COLEMAN
Lyrics by MICHAEL STEWART

BIGGER ISN'T BETTER

Music by CY COLEMAN
Lyrics by MICHAEL STEWART

OUT THERE

Music by CY COLEMAN
Lyrics by MICHAEL STEWART

Staying home, living day by day
Turning back should the highway bend,

may be safe but it
turning down ev-'ry

can't be duller,
chance you're given,

Seeing things only black and gray
Takes the risk out of life. and but

friend,

COME FOLLOW THE BAND

Music by CY COLEMAN
Lyrics by MICHAEL STEWART

BLACK AND WHITE

Music by CY COLEMAN
Lyrics by MICHAEL STEWART

THE PRINCE OF HUMBUG

Music by CY COLEMAN
Lyrics by MICHAEL STEWART

59

JOIN THE CIRCUS

Music by CY COLEMAN
Lyrics by MICHAEL STEWART

rats in - vade your at - tic and start leav - ing your ship._
sneeze, in - stead of bless you, you get jeers and a curse._
bank ac - count's a mil - lion, but it's all in the red._

Fol - low my tip,_ come a - way on a trip._ Just
Don't call a hearse_ while you still got the cherce._ Just
Don't lose your head,_ pin this note to the bed._ I've

Chorus:

Join The Cir - cus like you want - ed to
Join The Cir - cus like you meant _ to do
joined the cir - cus like I want - ed to